One Building In the Earth
New and Selected Poems

Maggie Helwig

Published by ECW PRESS
2120 Queen Street East, Suite 200, Toronto, Ontario, Canada M4E 1E2

NATIONAL LIBRARY OF CANADA CATALOGUING IN PUBLICATION DATA

Helwig, Maggie, 1961–
One Building in the Earth / Maggie Helwig
Poems.
A misFit Book

ISBN 1-55022-552-9

1. Title.
PS8565.E46O54 2002   C811´.54   C2002-902211-8
PR9199.3.H446O54 2002

A misFit book edited by Michael Holmes
Cover Photo: David Barker Maltby
Cover Design: Tania Craan
Cover Execution and Text Design: Darren Holmes
Production and Typesetting: Mary Bowness
Printing: Transcontinental

This book is set in Garamond and Univers

The publication of *One Building in the Earth* has been generously supported by the
Canada Council, the Ontario Arts Council, and the Government of Canada through
the Book Publishing Industry Development Program. Canada

DISTRIBUTION
CANADA: Jaguar Book Group, 100 Armstrong Avenue, Georgetown, ON L7G 5S4

PRINTED AND BOUND IN CANADA

ECW PRESS
ecwpress.com

One Building In the Earth
New and Selected Poems

Maggie Helwig

ecw press

CONTENTS

All Whom Flood Did Or Fire Shall O'erthrow
For David Barker Maltby, 1962-2001

It should not have been me at the end,
not me by your bed in a mask and a sterile gown;
it should have been someone
more valuable, consistent, someone whose love
was not confused with vanishing and poetry.

There could have been others, more brave and generous,
                                        who would not
have been in the same way afraid.
I was as random then
as I have always been, not who you chose but only
one who was there

And in the midst of this, these moments, seconds really,
the machines all around you, bright red blood on your lips,
I thought with surprise that your shoulders
had not been so broad; that you were, I was, older, a grownup.
You seemed so fragile when we met. But you had been alive.
Not dying.

Through hospital corridors like an initiate, every door
opening onto a deeper silence, the centre of a world
where your brain and blood lay down. Your body
a burning house, a high wall falling
at the edge of cold water

And we were young, dramatic, troubled,
our skin as smooth as milk or polished stone.
We drove along the highway in the afternoon — that day you gave me
a painted Pope in a plastic bag — and there was a restaurant
on a small hill, with snow around it, and the sunlight red on the snow,
and all the people in the car were laughing,
driving towards the night, this perfect moment `

I played harmonica in your darkroom, badly. I remember
broken tv sets, ribbons and pipes, paintings with dolls glued on.
The clear pale blue of your eyes.

Much later, I remember us
walking on a pier,
but I cannot think where it could have been, what lake, what harbour,
even what time.

David, the years.
It should have been someone other than me,
but I am selfish too, I will not give this up, this final parting.

A photograph, almost your last —
the man in the black coat, hunched and startled, against a brick wall.
A gas mask covers his face. His hand
grasps at a camera, and behind him
the curb is on fire, flame and cloud are rising.
I know that you took this picture, the man cannot be you,
but masked, anonymous, he
assimilates into your death. A casualty of some mysterious war.

I think of the distance you travelled. It could have been oceans.

It would not have been me that you called. This is,
I believe, the truth. I am trying
to tell the truth. But it happened this way at the end; I came.

David, the sharp bones of your face,
your elegance in layers of scruffy jackets,
the dark gold fall of your hair.

And no matter how hard I try I am turning this into a story.
There is no place to put this, no good word
as strict and unforgiving as fact, a stone on the shore.
There was blood on your mouth,
there was dark blood pooled at your ears.
You are dead.
Perhaps this is all I should be permitted to say.
(For a moment I thought — if I stop writing this I will lose you —

but that is a lie, I have already lost you, this is only
a mental construct, valueless, it is important
to remember this.)

Just one or two things that are simple. So many years ago
we walked down Spadina at two in the morning
and someone stopped us to ask directions. There was
nothing more to it than that. The yellow light on the street.

David, last month, it was spring, you turned in the doorway,
the shape of your life around you, a tangible thing.

There is some part of me
that waits on Bloor Street, the cold dusk falling,
to meet you at the corner.

SELECTED POEMS

summer solstice

city's crazy tonight   multicultural festival   saturday   and all that
      but
         quiet here

so many things to be remembered days and days of them all the time
write this down

daniel on his hands and knees under some steps
looking for one of the street people he tries to help out
or at least be company
he wasn't there though
and daniel and martin and me going to a yorkville restaurant two in
                                  the morning
giddy and giggling and half-angry and dumping apricot jam all over
                               our plates and
      walking off with most of a jar of it

bobby smiling

how I ended up walking around midnight through all these pine trees
        which are planted near the cn tower
        and the railway tracks   I was
        looking for an overpass or something
        thought it would be a good time to get kidnapped by a ufo
        but wasn't of course   as you had guessed

How the Angels Go All the Time
Breaking Your Heart

Well, we are maybe sitting in this bar
and the light blue angels come dancing out of the snow (and I am
always aware, when arms brush,
of the heat).
Also glasses of something bright orange.
It remains in the mind; we speak in our more
particular voices, humid.

I realize that in the end
the only hunger I understand is my own
and we are in the end quite alone
looking at each other, longing maybe,
wounded by angels, angel-known.

There is, though not here, this picture of some people.
It is chunky and sparse and curiously
disturbing. It is not, so to speak, a proper thing

because things should have no secrets. Objects are kind and do not lie
and I do not have to wonder
what they are thinking.

I do not know what you are thinking.

I do not know if sadness is the same to you
or need
and for all I know we are all
making it up. We are
alone on corners essentially, though
we breathe in a hot room; though we must hold

to orange half-light and the warm voices
which speak as if we knew each other
as if time or love or anything else
made us less than foreign, less

than terrible lost angels.

Poem from a Stolen Line

I will tell you many things
that were very picturesque
I will cup your
           face in my hands
         make you aware of your bones

This is a story about circles of yellow light on a porch
        or cups of coffee on a table   why there are so many
        shiny things — I will draw a figure
                on the backs of your hands   outline your eyes
                with my fingers

In a night full of chlorophyll and punctuation marks
we need not understand how we have been named or even know it.
        Separate, casual, indicative, existing
        I will smudge you with green.

Why the Bombs Keep Falling in Love

it's just how it keeps on happening
is what I'm thinking

and he says, you know why the bombs keep falling
in love with perfect passing strangers
and he says, there is no end to pain
you better go home
you better go home

it's just how people keep on being angry
and reading poetry and remembering how to kill

and he gets to the end of a sentence.
So he says real ironic, you know
how much it all matters, and why
the bricks will fall down on their knees then;
so he says, and I will hurt you because
that's the way it is, go on, this is not
where any of us belong.

And I am watching someone sitting on a stair
and I understand it all.

Why I Slept on the TTC,
for the People Who Asked

You can always sleep in the
        subway I said — it's something to do
and the saints have hair that glows in the dark
and switchblade feet   cutting up Christie Street — night.

Say there are these three people and they
      are imaginary people and they
      are walking along this corner.
And one feels guilty and one feels sick
      and one wants to sit down and freeze like a sidewalk
right there at Harbord and Huron where Lisa threw chairs.

Our violent prayers fall down like plastic oranges   purple
      hands (the subway
             is safer than houses   I don't
              feel so cold on the subway I said)
    o bless me
    while I sleep, lost saints with metal eyes.

You can always curl
      around a subway seat   you can always
      be safe in the subway I said   you can always

After Giorgio di Chirico

Women eat biscuits
and herring in oil
and look at their pieces of mail.
I, on the other hand, am a philosopher.

I have lived too long in this city, I can
no longer distinguish the sea.
All that will grow in the pavement is artichokes
and they have something like thorns.

My wife and my mother and Ariadne
weep in the morning, but by noon they
are too tired. My thighs and upper arms
are swollen like outer space.

Women eat biscuits
and herring in oil.
Today there was news of war.

Because the Gunman

Say in the terrorist's silvered second
we see escaping gateways, grace
and a lean and subtle desire; something here
revealing the city as a garden, doomed and green

because there is love that, purely in innocence, never happens
and we part
with a sadness almost impersonal.

Say that the lost dark eyes
which did not turn away in anger
but in circumstance, appear
on some internal street

because the gunman
in a rising moment, becomes
a dancer, and beautiful.

Geographical

The rocks and shadows of rocks
along the edges.
The rocks you can walk through if challenged. The shadows
are more difficult.
Imagine it like a plank fence in darkness, shining
with light from an empty window
and one bird calling.

There are no lakes, but certain places
shine like mercury.
Oranges grow, strawberries, pineapple
and a green fruit with marmalade flesh.
This by way of the rocks.

Those who come through the shadow
leave red handprints on the trees
and new wheat grows where they walk.

On the Observation of Clouds

The sky sun-daggered diagonal always, red and gold,
between the leaves they are thick
in clusters here and there
or feathered like the shapes of hands —

more strange at times.
Those
glossy as wing-backs, smooth and dark
as black slate mirrors

those hard and clear, and in appearance
near rose windows

those that split at times and fill the air
with drifts of seeds.

But it is said
they cast no shadows on the ground
or else at one time they did not, or again
will not until they gather

and there will be rain.

Preface

On the tongue of the dove
there is no way to speak; but say
that this is so.

Say you are walking on a point of sunrise
and your eyes are an orange horizon

or say, there is the light that turns
around the fingers of golden roofs in a city, green
that is not the accidental green
of pity and grass.

The wind passing clear over ribs
the fire in the seed, spires
of branches in the spine
the awful line of joy around your limbs. Speaking
fall of the golden blood.

Burning out of the falling word turn the cries
of the world naming

Or say
there are wings.

Chrysostom in Exile

All who are hungry, all who are fed by strangers, and the ones
who suck the scraps of flesh from delicate skeletons —
come, there are many fish, if it were not
so I would have told you, break the doors —
and in the bald salt wind
sniffling mucus, skinny
puts his hand on the bread that is our golden body.

This is our gift — that God speaks the fragrant
language of the poor, is one
with our saliva, muscles, enzymes, skin.
Who have waited, who have not waited
enter in.

The awful humility comes
like a flame on the city, and the gold ones there
fall on their knees.
In bald salt ripples
the consecrated flesh walks sweetly.
My dears
who have no repentance left, who distill
salt from your tears, who are to the night indifferent
come forward to the feast. The silver
wings of seraphs beat the air.

Pseudo-Dionysius the Areopagite
Comes to Dinner

You have to invite him, of course, that curious doctor.
He'd come if you didn't anyway
so you do.
You send him the printed card, or make a call
and tell all your guests to keep their windows clean
and be prepared.

One of those glassy nights in winter
stars clinking bright in the sky
and the snow like a lantern
he comes in his coat and enormous scarf

and steps from the taxi
in a thunder of horses.

Hands transparent round a glass of wine
the doctor addresses a radish —
"O ruthless root:
O thou self-nourishing core
red and white fruit of your flesh!
Consider, o radish, burning sphere,
thy circular clear and bitter feeding
on thine own sharpness, and thy fear;
and shed thy tears,
O solipsistic radish!"

After that
hors d'oeuvres are left untouched by everyone.

The wind sweeps down snow
like a fall-out of light. The house next door
is heavy with Christmas bulbs, blue and white.
Perhaps you think of roasting apples
by a fire.

Your fingers are cold, and your careful eyes
grow tired, and study
the folds of the beige and gentle curtain.

The clock is developing gaps
in the nature of freckles.

The doctor sits at the table
transubstantiates fish and lemon
mushrooms and toast.
Potatoes quiver at his touch.
Everyone clings to their placemats.

Doors flying open in every side of air
his skinny cheeks like mirrors, the doctor
falls with these succulent elements
through their daily passion
and lions leap out of his cutlery.

And having granted
life to new images
of pie and coffee, a last
absolution of your grace
the doctor rises from his place
reflected in the window, steps
into the spaces of the street
is gone.

Later, you wash the dishes.

Later, maybe, you clean out ashtrays
and bowls of peanuts.

You sit in a calm
and serious armchair
listen to music.
The curtains hang in beige confusion
the guests all stay in their rooms.

You count the world on your fingers.

Hunger and the Watchman: For Simone Weil

The only thing you know
is what you have to do. The only
thing you do is blind. To walk
the possible line of necessity.
It is winter in England.

Heat curls from windows and
you walk outside. When you have seen so much
become your fiction in your fixing love, the only thing
that you have left is that you have the chance to wait
for love that does not exist
being true.
This you must do.

If someone asks your name you can only say —
here is the point I watch at.

Attention.

The smoke in the English streets. The warmth
of pubs and steaming voices.
A tree.
A girl in red. To see
a thing entirely
is salvation. To see a man entirely
is to move
the possible hand of God.

Water-stained walls, the smell of sausage
on the damp air. The rats in France
an open sore on the leg of a boy
sun and a vineyard. Who sees you as you walk
the geometric streets?

Attention.
The salmon-coloured sky

grey water and wet stone.

To say, what are you suffering,
is the one true act of greatness we can own.

If you could fold your soul like leaves
and disappear.

Coughing in the English rain
too pale and far too thin, living
on cigarettes and headaches
standing in possible motion
on this non-existent line.

The only thing you do
is what you have to do. The only thing you know
is that it will be spring in England
when you die.

And the velvet-haired girl in Mayenne
in the valley of flowers, dark eyes
and tiny hands, blue flowers (and Achilles weeping
in a bronze mask, weeping
for his dead lover, beside the sea, and the women weeping)

the sun fine-grained and bright, and the pain came
immaculate, slicing the head at a blow
(the women stand
with their ankles in dirt, in the bronze masks, weeping)
the perfect
profile of trees scorching the brain like a torch, and the child
who should die were this
permissible, but
(and Achilles who ran so swiftly
could not sleep at night)
she searches, fingers in the dirt, the immaculate sea.
Definition. Oh. The soldiers are dying.

Therefore we weep for you
who have always been so gentle.

There is the long sound too of the sea
when it rakes over beaches always empty
despite the torches, under the deep moon
(les grands cimitières) and the dark holy women
the wives of the fishermen (shall we be slaves of the king?)
singing a song that was surely old
on the beach, in Portugal, the long sound.

Because it is red and slow-burning, because
the long plains of dead men, because at night
you walk in the land of no one, the long sound, because.

Mourn for the ruined cities, go to the ships.
There was this boy at Sitges, fifteen years old.
Somos atentos. Les grands cimitières.
Shall we be slaves of the king?

There were these women in Portugal, I
was by no means well, and the hymn was surely
very old. And I among others.
Carrying candles around the ships, we became on our knees.

I will speak to you now of the hunger.
I will say we are all
walking around like skeletons, starving
huge-eyed, paranoid
say we have lied and lied, painted ourselves with vile
imaginary bodies, denied
the pain the pain the pain

we must not we must refuse
to be satisfied with superficial
smiles and apples, I will not rest until I may
devour the garden, I will say
you know that the truth is the hollow
cheek and eye, you are all
so hungry you want to die do not deny it I
will cry what will I cry

And God, God, in Paris
the voices of men.
Pierre, his father was a farmer
who died. I have lain on the earth
too weak to stand, plucking at grapes.

The hands of men
are stained with juice and soil, with oil and blood.

I was very tired by the end.
That I will tell you.

I remember some days in Marseilles, that perfect winter
the light so pure and noble on the trees.
Sleeping on the floor, eating tomatoes and onions
I mastered the extremity of need.
I knew love.
It began to be hard to breathe.

The waters did not receive me
as a painted snake carried me to England.
Well.
All is well. I told them in the hospital
I would not be there long.
I thought, at the end, perhaps I could eat
some mashed potatoes the way my mother made them.
But the English, they do not know how.
Well.
All is well.

I would speak to you truly, I think.
I was terribly tired. You don't know.
I mean, I do not speak like this often, I would not —
well —
let us continue.

I was working in the factory. I had to put these pieces of copper in the furnace and take them out. Burned up to my shoulder at times. By the end of the day I could not control my movements. A man would jump up sometimes to pull the hood down for me.

The question of food remains a difficult one. Later I was working on the power presses. Did I tell you it was a Citroën factory? My conclusion is not that one should avoid love, but it is extraordinarily dangerous. Apart from all that, I should add that I find the machines themselves most interesting.

In June I drove a metal filing into my hand. I was frequently laid off. I do not think Lenin ever worked in a factory. Once, however, Trotsky hid in our house. André and I took him to see a film and they all got stuck in the elevator. The accident I spoke of was at the Renault plant.

One time somewhere else everyone was walking around singing the Internationale. I myself do not sing well, however.

(And here am I also, sitting
in a Toronto restaurant, crying, Simone, Simone.
Here, now, we are dying
of needing each other, dear dead sister
alone, alone, gripping electric-shock hands in the void
by the bright red exit sign and the radio trees

Sitting in Toronto, crying.

This
is not poetry, this is not
what I call poetry, this is the demon Hunger.
My dear, my dear
I will cry for your torture here in Toronto.
Clutching, your pain, electric light,
listen, the blaze in the darkness —

Simone, Simone)

What it comes down to. What it comes down to. I mean, that we cannot lie about it. And our lips so terribly burned. Whipped through the city. We love like cannibals. We are a huge walking famine. We view from a distance the beings as essential to us as food, this is a miracle of horror, our greatest tragedy is that we cannot eat God. At times he would fall silent, take some bread from a cupboard, and we would share it. This bread really had the taste of bread. I have never found that taste again. Strange. That the words should come so hard. We want to see the flowers. Turkey, Christmas pudding, Easter eggs, marrons glacés. These constitute the real meaning of the festival. Milarepa's discovery, food is the irreducible element, proof of the reality of the universe. Reality is not to be had cheaply. Eat me, drink me, eat me.

The nightmare, becoming.
Germany, Poland, the barbed wire, the trains
starving, starving, the skeletal babies,
the women with withered breasts
the awful eyes of hunger behind the wire
soul-eater, the death-bodies, the Nazi laugh.

The children eating rats and dung in the ghetto.

The Jewish girl in London, the French child
far away from home, coughing
staring through windows, skinny, exhausted, unknowing.

The world's death body, death dream, our hunger
carved in human flesh.

Watchman, what of the night?

What of the slick light that flickers on faces in lonely streets?
What of the dark sleep of slaves, mindless and torn?
And why do we ever come to God except mere hunger?
Pierre and René and I
we would watch the dawn rise in Les Halles
women in evening gowns coming to eat fried potatoes.
Slick streets, cigarettes, the keeping of silence
the voices of men.

Watchman, what of the night?

I wake at the window, walking, smoking.

The night in Spain, in the war
I stumbled, plunged my leg in boiling oil for cooking
and for hours I shook with cold, the darkness flaring.
We love like cannibals.

The way the light drips down the sky in the finally morning.

Standing here, waiting, shaking with hunger
on watch, slick as a bayonet, oh —
Pierre, what —
Simone, what of the night?

These are some of the persons I have known. My brother André. Simone Petrement. Pierre Letellier, I knew somewhat. René Chateau. Boris Souvaine. Auguste Detouf. Maurice Schumann. Joë Bousquet. Gustave Thibon. Many of these persons, of course, I have not heard from for some years.

My landlady here is Mrs Francis. She is, I believe, very kind. There are few in London to visit me in the hospital but that is surely not their fault. My parents, of course, must not know that I am ill. They love me very much, it is not good for me to see them.

I have attained a degree of detachment, but it is a result of exhaustion and is a purely biological process. As such, it has no value.

Distance seems to me the very essence of friendship.

I should very much like to eat a piece of chocolate, but one must not, of course, be absurd.

Small one, Simone-Adolphine,
may you have flowers. Blue French flowers, may they fall
on your thin hands.
(And this, I know, is sentimental. Mrs Francis
throwing the little tricolour bouquet into the grave.
Silly, female, British. All is well.)
Velvet-eyed child with midnight hair
laughing in forests.

Sister, I give you what I can.
Pray for me, sister.

Beautiful child, will you sing?

The Other Variations

*I found I was dissatisfied with my earlier recording, which
presents a series of thirty brilliant but independently-minded
variations ... I felt I had discovered a certain underlying unity,
a sort of mathematical correspondence ...*

— *Glenn Gould*

And the voice said: Cry.
And I said, what shall I cry?
Surely the people is grass.

There is no answer to
the scattered limbs, the arms
too short or else too long, the huddled
shoulders, failing ear and eye.
The head must bend
to the creature. Say that this
may be a reverence —
or not.

Finally, you must look at it
alone. The keyboard
is no final help. We are not speaking
of a thing.

The gardens we remember — cross
the stream in the ravine —
are very dry, oh son of man,
and music which may bring you sleep
is a boy's music, not the fugues
that torment the insomniac wolves.
The Russian winter grows
mysterious trees, that bear
metallic fruit.

The miscellaneous pieces that
are not a life — the things

that kept me, stencilled me on lines.
I try
to eat as little as I can, and to retain
each thing distinct.

The easy ambiguous compounds
lie on the skeleton, bags of potato chips
and Molson's bottles on the tundra.
But over it the wind begins
to burn the lips like coals of fire.

There is a terrible space between
a child and a child, which we will only cross
with hands raised up to strike, with rocks.
Will the music move
across the terror?

In my logical desert, this
Toronto where I am, the savage children
never left me. I have wept
and cried out from the ground

leaning in the direction of the cross.

The notes
pass notes behind the back of the music.
The dance continues — listen —
am I speaking secrets
to my own blunt ears?

I have not stopped dreaming of autumn. The fear
has not diminished, the leaves
the innocent leaves are hammered to the stone.
Nothing is known.

I have not tied the nerves' split ends,
the noises in the head — if I have said
that I had found my way
I lied. I am subjective, sensual, am

not silent
am not saved. How long?

The hermit in the Russian night
was sick, and crippled later,
and he died.

The waves will always
break like waves, and part
to release the light, but I
ride boats no longer, and
if hand strikes hand, it still
involves a self-involving hand.

But at a point
between reflecting eyes —
stand still.

I will admit
the fish are not in need of saviours, I cannot
be other than I am, and that
transcendence holds a necessary blindness.
When
you cannot say 'this thing' or 'then'
you must be where you are

where one
is neither means nor end
but only music.

One moves across the keys until
the key is lost, and every thing
becomes a mystery

and we are part, I guess, of all
anonymous people. Guilt is also
part of music, and of mercy too.

Arabesque, the delicate
chain of voices, the fugue entwines
the bars across our eyes, the tactile
ornament of our lives

the coloured glass and candles. There
will not be peace.
In this we find our rest,

perhaps.
I doubt
if this is best, but we are here
in a home we cannot see.

I wasted time, and now does time waste me —
no more.

One walks in Toronto, and I would not say
that I am happy here, but once I saw
the weird belled flower of a cactus. Events
are never one thing only, there is joy.

Over the signatures, singing
in harmonic flow, suspended, transient
and unknowing always —
cantilena
over our fevers.

On a round planet, one may say
that night goes on forever; somewhere, then,
the northern dawn is burning
like a phantom curtain

and the blurred dynamic of our movements
is a secret we have understood
when we are sleeping.

We never own
our memories or our futures, and we do not know
what we might mean to say,
but still we say it.

The mystery of communication
is that it is possible. This is the nursery rhyme
that explodes in the eye.

And I said, what shall I cry?
And the voice said:
Cry.

Moving/apart

There is no degree of love that does not
make us more alone.

But the silence will endlessly save us, all the Saint Gregorys
singing in the come-oh-come gentle of the night,
We know nothing.
Only to say, the air is fast, here at the curb;
the air is fast, and I cannot ask any person
to climb these neon distances with me.

Okay.

I cannot speak simply today, dwelling
in this baroque silence, the complex leaving and taking
of my decimal heart, coded desires
and lack of desires
and end of desire
and so forth. All the Saint Johns
and their electric violins
in the speeding air. *I love you,* I say to the curb, *you are
the end of all seeking.* There is no reason
this should not be true.

You.

The always second person, the urgent word
that orbits indifferent day to day between
saviour and lover and lovely stranger
and the terrible ones so close to us
we are no longer sure of their names.

Because I prize it all, the alibis
that the heart creates and
the falcon hath stoln my make away and
you would not think to look at him but
he was famous long ago.
And myself the later Magdalene, starving on the rock and amazed
at the secret stupidity of the love
we so vastly need.
The perfect lost assumed implicit *you*.

And the bloodstreams we move in.

Each of us dreaming the other,
sweeping the floors as the floors weep silver,
knowing we cannot be less than a part, as we do not
go away, we only keep going.
We turn with our desperate hearts,
this old dance.

At dawn . . .

At dawn you lie in your bed
shaking and crying, and all you can pray
is *please let me help and make it all right*
and *please* and *please.*

If I could take these broken hearts
and rock them to sleep in my arms. If I could
give to us all one moment of peace
on the highway at night, in a warm place;
the light of small grass, the clean grass, darling, sleep.

This is a love song, this is not
for anybody new. Let the dead rise. Let perfect strangers
walk through the house with armloads of bricks
unfurl their giant blue and white flags
lay carpet on the corners of the streets.
Let the saints put raisins and hazelnuts
at our difficult feet.

Under the arc of sadness as
the sun and dark roll over
there is nothing I have but a finite number of words
and the wish I could tell you, *give me your pain
I will take your pain, I will carry it for you
to the subway and the store.*
Let the skies open. Let the silver fish
swim in white rivers, let the rain
walk like a kitten on your skin.

Strangers who breathe like each other, we hold our hands
at a distance against imaginary glass —
but oh, I wish you all the best;
trembling in bed in the morning, let the light fall
and lie down beside you and rest.

Joseph of Arimathea or so

Me and my bad shoes in the rain
and cars passing soft
like all of us dead and wounded bodies quietly falling
into each other's arms.
And the sugar nails that hold us to these bad hills, I will pull them
out of your hands with my teeth.

I have said this often enough before —
we have nothing to share but a coat or two, possibly
rides in a car.
But Joseph the stranger, he was rich
and a good man in his way
and in the twenty-four hour convenience store
the utter light and silence amazes my eyes.
My dear ones.
In secret I will kiss
your sugar wounds.

On the bad hills we walk up and down
and it is not difficult, nothing is difficult
and the sweet ocean is near.
I shall be cared for by strangers, and this
shall be love in a sort of perfect form and
we are not ones who last for long
and our Joseph lovers
wrap us in good night.

Graffiti for J.J. Harper

BELIEVE IN
THE LORD JESUS
OR YOU WILL BE
<u>DAMNED</u> ETERNALY
AND PEOPLE WITHOUT
SOULS
WILL TORMENT YOU
AT THE END OF TIME

The black ice keeps breaking, it is
how the black ice keeps breaking, it is
the cardboard angels lashed to rocks with wire.
Do the dead suspect, do they rip black plaster
away from their softening arms legs kidneys fingernails eyes?
God the Propellor spins at the tip of our heads
festooned with bits of skin and private spies.

And we all begin in more or less to know the dead
to love them at night, to follow them by day
through the streets of a cold country, the quick flash
out of our fear in the March break ice
(oh the dark is too dear and it builds its nests
in our throat and wrists we are so
afraid to be here)

And he is one, and he is one
and I am a half
complicit kid from the city
and he is dead.

God the Propellor slices our brains for a lucky charm
and spins us into our frozen un-
certain blood, poor stupid immigrants
and the bodies fall warm on us at night
the black muck of their bones.

Microdot nephews and nieces on our television feet
we crunch over snowdrifts, lost, out of
all connects between the pieces, in
addition
angry at something inside these bodies
precious our pain. And he
rests his chin on the fist of a nightstick
and I wear a chain of paperclips on my arm
and he is dead.
And God the Accident crashes in traffic (if
our bones were bread, if our bones were bread . . .)

This is my body, says. Come take.

After   Constable Cross grabbed Mr.
                    Harper's arm   the
constable's
          revolver went off, killing   Mr. Harper.
He
          pulled on Mr. Harper's arm.   Constable
                    Cross was admitted
          to hospital Tuesday night.   Constable Cross
is receiving a daily dose of
          50 milligrams of Valium the maximum
          recommended level is 30 milligrams
                    Constable   Cross   six days
          after the incident   in a video   acted
out   his   part
                    dressed on the tape in jeans and a t-shirt
          Constable Cross   spoke coherently but sometimes
               was unable to understand simple questions
          before a packed audience Constable
                    Cross seemed agitated   when cross-
                                        examined
                    Another officer played
Mr. Harper   Constable Cross   has been admitted
          to hospital several times since
          the shooting
"I remember a bang, a flash, and where my hands were"
          The bullet
                    ripped through an artery above Mr.
Harper's
                    heart   Valium causes
                    bleeding in an artery over the heart
"I happened to reach for my gun. I pulled the trigger."
          Constable Cross experiences
anxiety attacks headaches insomnia vomiting facial
          twitches
The officer playing Mr. Harper
          stood erect and backed away, acting
as if shot

46

                Constable Cross said
officers told a racial joke after the shooting he
                said they
told the joke to make him feel better Constable
                Cross pulled on Mr. Harper's arm
                Mr. Harper was the director
                of the Island Lake Tribal Council
                        Constable Cross
                        fired his revolver Mr. Harper
                stood up, stepped back and sank to the ground.
In
the video
        another officer plays the part of Mr. Harper
                Constable Cross   spoke of the merits
                of suicide. There is
        no record of questions asked by Sergeant
Williams

                                                                                of

Constable Cross
                                he could not recall
                some of the details   he acted out
                        his part in the tape
                Another witness broke down he had
                        rewritten his notes
                                Constable
                                Cross
                encountered a man in a nearby street

                                "It's not like on TV.
                                It's a bad feeling."

CIA LANDLORD

DRUGS INOSENT
TENANTS!

ALL THE PEOPLE
ON THIS
STREET

ARE CIA!

The green tree bends
in the cold zone
and the paranoid grass
in the cold zone
our also chant creates
   let call
 the spirits of shiny cars, of metal numbers
 that screw onto our houses, let call
 our coat-hanger bodies, our loss
 the wheels of the cold zone turning, microdot, we
 would locate ourselves, truly we do not want
 to kill any more, let call
the tree is bitter green and we
are missing selves in the paranoid zone and he
is bleeding from a vein above his heart
and he appears as a dot on our table
and I try to adore the city into life and I can't
and he

the green tree bends
our also chant creates
to find
the lyric somewhere, blood in the root of the cross
   revolver flash
   we are so afraid
   we are made into dots and silver

it is too hard to love when these things happen
try and tell us
something we don't know

in the cold zone

The inquiry was preparing
        to call Inspector Dowson at midmorning
when
Inspector Dowson was a central
    figure in the Harper case   Inspector
Dowson
he also had access to the physical evidence
        was discovered, the inquiry was postponed
    waited until his wife and children were out of
the
    house
he instructed the officers
        who questioned Constable Cross
Inspector Dowson   a senior Winnipeg police
officer
        just hours before his scheduled testimony
adjourned abruptly when it was discovered
        he did not testify last year
to resume in the first week
 of October   Inspector Dow-
son
            in the basement of his Winnipeg home
            his own service revolver
            a single gunshot
the atmosphere surrounding the inquiry
        Inspector Dowson   Mr. Harper

EVIL PROPAGANDA
TRANSMITTED INTO MIND
BY RADAR
BRAIN
WAVES

no sweep of rain

over and over we learn this world of our very own, the way
it does not wish that we should care
that no one will ever permit you to love, that you try again
and it will never work
that the blades of God will slice your flesh and not God or anyone
will love you back on earth

and you say at last oh well
you might as well —

And he has said it, the quick flash in the frozen zone
and the other falls, the blood above the heart.
And he has said it and lied and made himself
endlessly alone.
And I have said it too I guess
and resigned too many people into a kind of grey, I say to myself
you cannot just hurt forever.

And he is dead.

We call them the dead because they are dead.
Remember this, it is not pretend
and the end of all this is nowhere in sight.

There will be no help for us, learning this world
so as not to kill, in the hands of God the Condition of Pain
but I have to walk at it again, I have to
walk there again, with a chain of paperclips
no rain
and every connection cut still beating heart

THE WIND IS MEASURED AND EXACTING

NOW STAY IN REALITY

And he is dead
and he is dead
and he is dead
and I am nothing much
in the face of the long hate, praying for un-
identified flying souls, knowing there is blame
and let understand, *eleison,* mercy
God the Propellor
God the Accident
God the Condition of Pain.

It is not in our interest to disclose.
This has gone on too long.
(and oh when you break open the grass is sweet
and the lights on the street will feed you like syrup)
It is not in our interest.
The man fell bleeding into the crunchy snow, that is all you know
where the hands are
the cross, we must learn this world on death's metal rail.

Bring us to life in the paranoid zone.

How Can I Tell You That the World Is Round

Thirteen million burning tires
blast waves of poison into the air near Hamilton,
plastics, benzene, black smoke.
They are clearing a twenty-mile path, thirteen million tires
spontaneously ignited, they were
filled with a desperate joy.
They transcend their condition.
They burn.

The glory of the Lord
is risen upon thee.

And though he come in poison
though he come
and in black smoke *(shine shine)* and though —
here will we bless, and there, and in the thirteen
million burning tires, *oh dance.*

The red plastic angels untangle their wings from the dark
and bob in front of your face, they say, *Indeed,*
it is true, we have seen it, we
believe these things.

shine shine oh new jerusalem etcetera

The scribble skins from your fingers onto
all flat surfaces, vivid (and someone
scrawled CANALETTO
HEEBEL SMIRT
in a copy of the Alexiad
and I carried it with me for years like a map
or a key) *re-*
joice, oh you.

I mean — this possibility of happiness, of
a simple and not dematerializing tree or thing —
(I guess you can change; the wild bright paint on the Berlin Wall
and the Wall coming down)
(I guess you can change)

And it is still true of course that young women with pretty hair
have been bullied by cops and lovers
and it hurts for real when you're kicked and things
go frequently bad
but we do paint our colours onto the air
we do exist there.

We are without hope and beautiful.
We are in the middle of the sky, we do not know
where we begin and end.
And absolute freedom is cold as fear
but it will be all right, my dear,
it will be all right
(at the first turning of the second stair   )
This is the place you come to, we are
the dwellers in that country.

The colour of any desperate afternoon,
reading every label in the corner store because there is nothing more
your life is worth —
nobody else can save you, but listen
there is a trick in this, it is not
what it only means.
This is the land inside the fire.

How can I tell you that the world is round,
humility is endless, and it rains?
People in doorways are crashing into the light
against wet sidewalks, and the night
goes on like fabric.

Come from that scene, all you. And.
I am starting to understand, you see,
that we are simply real.

The Last History of Byzantium

I
The emperor is bent upon a field of gold and where
they tore his eyes out there are rubies.

The city empties under his slender
platinum hands. The lambs
walk out of the golden city to the cross, it is named
jerusalem bethlehem city.

The emperor bends like a bird, blind bleeding
a jewel on his ripped white face and the waves
call hollow to the fading lambs.
The city empties like water under his hands.

II

Holy Sophia took my eyes
for the face of Judas. I am content
for I am the secret historian of the city.
And Holy Sophia took my wrists
to bleed on the emperor's floor and I
do not protest.
And Holy Sophia took my lungs
to be eaten by doves in the market — let this thing be done.
For who can speak of true or false
in the high places of Byzantium?

Many go blind in Byzantium.
It is the gold and the sea.

III
The sun melts your bones at the city's edge
and the moon turns black, it is only a lie.
I am watching.
The emperor takes off his head and walks through the halls.

Theodora, lovely witch,
is eating herself from the inside out
bright teeth creeping through
her blackening flesh.

have mercy lord.

I am writing the histories, I am a child
of incense and sin.
One king will die by drowning, one by fear
and Rome will fall from all the high places
and from the outside in
and one king slender as love will stand
in a white robe, in a cloud of gold and blood
and disappear.

IV
The saints will come out of the desert
crawling in their great chains, or blind, or pierced with thorns
and from their four directions one by one
to gather in the golden city they will come.

With fragile bones and bleeding eyes
they will go through the broad streets, past the great towers of
                                                                Byzantium
walking under a copper sun
silencing murmurs of caged birds, rumours of wars.

The saints will come out of the desert
stand in the marketplace while all the doors
open, and the city
meets them there and rings them round.
And in their terrible rags they will lift their arms and cry
and the city will shimmer and fold
like a gold-leaf curtain to the ground.

Then the quiet wind will blow around the weeping saints
and rain fall gentle on their sores.

V

The emperor under the water
arms folded across his linen chest
green plastic over his eyes.
The wind is a suicide torpedo
on the far islands.

And the sapphire surges and crashes over the dead
daggered with gold on the round roof of the tomb, and the font
where we drown, go down, catacomb.
And the ancient king face down in the pool.
But I am the historian, bleeding
on your carpet, I will take
these things in an incense cloud and make them
be one thing, and true.

Bits of the dead come up out of the water.
May these bones.
Holy Sophia, *you.*

VI

The black eyes of Sophia, the wild curve of light blasting
upwards, the dome, she is standing
slender, black, between the king of battle and the king of law. Sophia
eats my heart in the market, she is the history.

The kings came from a dry, an older city to Byzantium, as
did I; our small
and bitter sun is dark at the centre.

The fierce green of the fields, the emperor
bends beneath the mist to say that Rome is gone.
Sophia, the lambs are crashing through the cross
into your gold black arms.

VII
Slashed at the wrist, I crouch and compose
on the purple imperial floor.
To the saints who weep at my doorstep — I am
not in the best of health, I am not
entirely well. Under the sun
we fry our souls on the sidewalk; oh saints, beware.
My colour is not good, I am always tired.
Go in good light.
To the bearkeeper's daughter — you lovely death,
dancer, the earth is also flesh.

Three fingers in blood and three in holy water,
emperor, brother poison, we breathe
together at last, into the dark.
The sky goes rotten, mushroom grey.
I could sleep.
Beautiful earth, your skin is silk
and our robes are always gold.

VIII
and kings and christian sailors, dear, for you

The dervish night
moves lips across my skin, tongue into wetness; if you then
do love the damage, holy sweet Sophia, come beside me
into our disaster.

Do eat my lungs and liver, save me, burn my heart forever
but do not bless the wreckage, do not praise
this rotten sky.

Sophia love, Sophia lord
historian I

IX

The emperor stands at the gate, he is almost like day
and explosives blast the great wall and he would
turn into a dove and fly away,
the last great illusionist of Byzantium —

and the ships are too late, at the gate
he raises his sickle-moon sword — smoke on the city, gold, gold.

The emperor arches, gold and precious stones, the emperor
bends, stands, his black blood rubies, god yes there is pain —

under his slender plutonium hands
the city empties like rain.

In Time of Danger

Because the world burns I collect information,
file and crossfile, believing salvation finally lies
in the hands of librarians. Late at night
we click on the red lights of the machine
and the microchips whisper their intimate suggestions
of anthrax, oil and hunger.

I walk in the snow with my arms stretched out, make
these deliberate traces, this is my name, walk here, it will be as if
we had spoken face to face.
I leave in your shoes invisible bits of paper
that mention easter.
I say to the light, astonish me now
in these green fields of Toronto.

Damage in time of danger grows
like a tree of ice
and I bless the winter that makes all things distinct.
Because the world burns. Because the oil is crawling
through the water and the air, and starving people hide at borders
under a dozen different guns.

I note every fall of the data chips (and am myself
a random piece of information, moderately displaced,
without a context that makes much sense), turn out the lights
and watch the computer screen glow.
I become accustomed to languages that are private
to myself alone, and on the other hand plant tiny
codes in the files, just to say I was here, hey, I was here.

Memory leaps at unexpected moments
while the bodies fall
walking into the forty days
after forty days of war.
So meet me in the desert, brother snake, and there will be
nothing we need to say to each other, only this.

On the bare hill where garden vegetables
burst into flames, mysteriously saved,
and there is no information to exchange, simply
being as present and notable as cold water,

and I wonder — if the angels catch you, do your pains
cut wounds like jagged metal in their chests? Are we ever
                                        innocent of
our terrible pains?

The secret name of safety . . .

the secret name of safety in
a state of transit. on the night bus again
between these cities — say,
a mystic's dangerous sister,
head shaved and hollow-cheeked, offering up my veins
in a number of senses.
drifting toward the vision. here, without
location, again.

enchanted by renunciation and the loss of blood
breathing in the hallway
while the priests like crazy men throw handfuls
of water into the air, shining like gold
(or say, she is simply riding the bus all the time
between the two points of her soul)
the mystic's nameless sister, least of the children
brushing the gates of the kingdom with my cramped feet.

and Sarajevo burning.
and Los Angeles burning.
and the scorch on my hand when I touch the glass of the window
being in motion
being invisibly guided through dangerous roads.

or consider yourself as waking up
on a cold uranium morning
and try to tell me we do not defy belief
that our life is not astonished and loyal
to this awkward flesh, the incompetent shining of our loves,
God's younger cousins, x-rayed by sunlight.

(she is only a moment between the particles
descending
and the moments on the stairway,
on the highway, alive.
she is only this movement, a girl in a boat,
as golden as anyone else)
our breath in transit, the secret
name of peace.

Human Hearts

*"East Timor, February 1992 — Evidence of massacres after
November 12 continues to mount ... Witnesses report that, after
a heavy rain on November 28, a box containing twenty human
hearts was found in the river near the hospital ... it is believed
that the bodies of a number of victims were cremated at the
hospital ..."*

Only the human hearts, harder than fire.
Only the stubborn impossible human hearts.

We stumble up from the side of the river
heavy with rain and blood (oh mother
we did not ask to be here   we only wanted
to live some simple life   oh mother we did not ask)

and the girl at the river weeping.

We die still trying to explain, *I never meant
to cause you any pain, I never meant
to make you worry — only this is
the single thing to do.*

And the human hearts float up in the water.

A heart is a difficult thing to burn.
It only goes black and hard,
dangerous stone. The human muscle bends,
clenches and dances against the bone, the human skin
may break and join again or break forever, but
a heart is a thing too hard to burn.

(and here in my winter country, my vein
collapsing at the needle's point, bubble of blood in my hand, I say
I would never wish to cause you pain
but go ahead despite)

The sea collides with the burnt green shore
the human skin
puckers under the water, melts
into the sand, bubbles of blood
in our awkward human hands, like the human
heart of God. Like the
muscle and bone of God on our burning tongues.
The cars turn around in the narrow street. The teenage soldiers
mark patterns of death as intricate as lace
with their bayonets' points. Blood bubbles and clots
on the scorched-down ground.

We die in soft confusion, we die
explaining the hard conditions of love, we die
in silence, or we do not die but come instead
to this new home of the bodies, the heart,
the bone of the jaw, the pit of the eye.

The human girl who weeps.

oh mother we do not want to live this way

These hard, implacable
these desperate human hearts.

Trouble in the Graveyard

*"We don't want any more trouble in the graveyard," the
Indonesian soldier said.*

Because all space is curved I will wait.
I will sit in a chair in my room and wait.
I will eat crackers and coffee and apples,
dressed in a scarf and a white shirt, waves at my eyes,
while the universe goes on bending and God
falls like a spray of water and dies
and wakes on a hillside, waiting too;
as all the numbers we know keep waving goodbye
to planets falling
into hot space, and we
keep falling as well, soft creatures full
of guilt and damage and fugitive grace.
Because time is a spiral, and space and love are curved,
I save as one must the dear lost bodies of strangers
in the memories of my skin and spine.

I believe all falling things will live forever. I
believe in the innocence of falling things.

This is a night about the laws of speed and matter.
This is a night of projectiles and gravity
and the teenage prophets in love and trouble in the graveyards.
I believe you can walk off a cliff and keep on walking. I have
done it every day for years. It is never easy
and you sometimes forget
but you never hit the ground.

My love, I need you like the night
needs falling creatures, like
the body of God needs trouble and faith and the silk touch of skin.
I have been remaking space
from direction and distance and the curve of your arms,
constructing

desire towards the morning (towards
the rush of air on every side, the outline of hands, the act of a name).

I love you as
light loves the air, as I travel through darkness,
as I love your mouth, your hands, your hair, as we create
memories of the beloved dead in our tangled bodies,
space for the sudden someday news
of incredible change, of how the world
will never end.

Believing
that troublesome beauties will rise again
in the fierce need of the living, believing
all perfect broken things are not abandoned
in the days of children and bullets —
I begin with a word
and wait for trouble in the graveyard.

You in the Morning

Given that light is a paradox which
should not exist as it does, given
that the sun will kill us all in the end, and the lucid
eggshells of air are full of our very own danger,
still you in the morning are beautiful. And I allow
that space is curved
and perhaps we have no choices, only
implacable grace and the laws of physics and the fast arc of radium,
that skin is a chemical and
we can avoid neither salvation nor solitude.
Accepting then,
I will fall beside you for a time
in this cascade of particles, will say
that tongue against tongue we shall believe in language, the random
acts of speech and love.

Given that in a bending universe nothing ends
except particular worlds, still I insist
on saying your name in the morning, the ways
we make each other finite and forever, falling
into this bright impossibility, wave and particle, creatures in flight,
because death exists, but also because
of you in the morning.

NEW POEMS

Variations on Spring

I

April again.

A woman with black hair
rides her bicycle round and round the park, hanging
onto the fence with one hand.
High narrow walls in the dangerous spring.

If the sky could be tied down with ropes and flowers, still
that would not mean that I could sleep.
There is no such thing as somewhere else, there are
no excuses for love or oxygen.

If the veins in my temples are made
of honey and sand, melting in sudden heat or the nervous
alarm in the bones of my shoulder; if I am here
in the midst of faces trimmed with loss and lace;
this means, I guess,
there are only particular choices.
To touch at a distance these sad fantastic strangers
to be in this place
to see straight through to the laws of motion
at six in the afternoon in the fiercely articulate air.

Spring ghosts like scraps of fabric drift in winds, I am
forever possessed by glass and the jagged
borders of fragile things.

II

These red flowers, the shock
of recognition, blood on the hand.
In the puzzle of streets, shiny with slick ceramic tiles
(green lemon white and the sea)
women and men, red flowers. It is
like the same story, falling and rising,
how we are all a part of it
how we will smash the walls of the prison, the bad bones of fear.

The sea is filled with soft creatures, their flesh
full of salt and chemicals, their white bodies loose,
spreading on secret constructions of mineral.
And we no less difficult (salt in our blood, our hearts
                                        surrounded by water)
swim in our deep dreams, rocked in rich darkness,
tell the same story, shaping it under our fingers,
red petals, complicity, love.

III

Tell me, I say, about bright rags
or pale blue dresses in the traffic on Brixton Road
coffee and basil
the heat of spring on my back and the noise of bent steel.
Tell me true dangers, actual holes
in the spaces of April, wild seconds of freedom
careening round a corner, into cold magnificent grace.

Light falls on lilac. Upturned hands
swallow enzyme and sun, and I
small person in transit, in a Chinese jacket,
am here between the lyric windows
purple jam bleeding onto white bread
vanishing things.
In this place, this second season.

Electric children, powered by definitions
rust on Walworth metal
the movement of rivers and milk in our green dreaming.

August 6, Novi Sad

Soldiers and stones by the river of our bad dreams,
and deep in the warm night the water in our bones
makes us too beautiful too endure.
We send these bright rags and tatters, torn from our hearts
into the darkness, the rich waves, the black light.

I know that everything, in the end,
must go from my hands into this river
from this fragile lantern of my skin
asking why we are all so perfect and blind
what our bodies look like in the dark
as our bad imaginations manufacture time.

In the dreams of hate too many real bones are breaking open, spilling
water and blood and marrow on the hot streets, too many
real shattered beautiful girls are falling. The world explodes
like a day in summer. Make gentle the souls of the dead.

The living are walking, one by one, down metal stairs, down sand,
light in our living hands
night in our living eyes.

I am a bad thought at dawn, my fingers clenched
in the morning's line of fire, believing more
in rain and darkness. My feet in wet sand
by a broken boat, wrapped in the water's green smell
I believe them now, these walking flames.
Wash the bad names from this river
rock in our small arms the hungry ghosts
in their lost places of velvet and lead, all our poor hearts.

We let go our holy things
scraps of bright hair, language, apples
fall into darkness
fall
the most lovely wounded creatures in the world.

The City on Wednesday

The street at six in the morning
moves in the darkness as knowledge moves in our bodies, blind
the hum and transit through passages of night.
We could not be more alone.
Each of us, dark travellers, me who sits on the bed
at the window in a cold dawn, watching.

The lines of the city extend like bones through space,
not asking for directions, burned by the wind.
But in this cold blue moment I am
not so afraid as I might have been
alone, now, here.

Things fall from us, I mean
when our hands are empty, when our eyes are sore
and our hearts imperfect;
until we are wrapped in the comfort of morning
soft children cuddled in blankets of light and sleep.

In the morning, grapes in my cupped hand, green,
pale with water and faith.
The sun floods Walworth Road. The city on Wednesday
abandons itself to trust, to the constant hope
of bright-coloured paper, wool and cotton, complexity.
The gifts of the spirit that fall down around us
like tiny wheels and tops and flags, red plastic kites
and the smoke that drifts upward from the cardboard burning in
                                            the yard next door,
our journeys to the banks of the river.

At noon I pause, in the sun, at a point in the air
and my body aspires upwards. We have
no other way through the city.

Moments fall onto the road . . .

Moments fall onto the road like water. This is all
impossibly true. It is all
danger and need, you know that the desert
is rarely dry, that the broken thin people in t-shirts and plastic sheets
struggle through mud and disease. That our skin must shiver with pain.
And you cannot deny this other thing too,
that a rain of wild roses pours down on the sunlit city
scarlet and purple, violets, mustard and cinnamon. You
cannot pretend that any of this is not true.
Your lover's tongue inside you at the heart of a red sphere
the perilous edge of the day
and the damp sick dying children, your heart
contains these things.

A woman, aging, cared-for, neat
screaming outside the doors of justice in a glare of light.
And the days through Saint Gregory's darkness, dizzy, blind,
into a riot of colour, bells and fruit,
scarlet and linen surrounding your tearing chest.

Because we are here.
Because the sight of any one of us could make the sun
drop dead in the street, amazed, we are warm, we are singing.
There is blood at our doorways, blood on our feet
but we are, we are still, in this wet, this breeding desert.

You may spend days in sunlight, shaking, sick,
frail as an ivory saint with broken nails, you may be
responsible at times for life and death.
None of this changes. None of this
makes it change.

Listen, the lights come on in the dark blue city,
listen, the wind shifts direction, you are not innocent, you are not
free of fear; but you are moving. There is sugar and cream on your lips
there is evidence scratched in the tips of your fingers, there is
possibility in this place, in your body, here.

South America — Nativity

I

All things are gathering
under this warm rain. We lean, our hands like rose-coloured wax,
in the arms of the trees, the water's surface shaken,
small red birds, blue birds.
This first day of this week, this season.

Cross-legged on the bed, slices of over-ripe fruit
melting like perfume, fresh bread
dried flowers in tiny boxes, scraps of paper, the longing for distance.

All things are coming together.
Stalls in the market sell butter and fish and *candomblé*
the prophecy candle's purple light surrounds us sleeping.
We are small figures, journeying.
We wait for the arrival of ourselves.

In a village a boy rides a bicycle, slantwise,
skidding, down gravel roads. All things
are in one place.

II
In the sand-coloured stone, elegant, silent,
the knowledge of the city
stands in its proper speech, in words
like heat and contemplation, these streets informed.
Ciudad vieja, we are slight letters in this time
in search of a mythical market, memory at the top of a hill,
among the tomatoes and bright ephemeral windows.
Flesh burns at the edge of the sea.

Girl in a blue dress, turning,
in the heart of a shower of silver; cafés and murals, signs.
I would learn my intention from the stone streets of the city
at the feet of the long water, incandescent,
exiles and immigrants, scratching at the shore, this story.
The new world was not meant for sleep or hunger.

I mean — what we must know is never clear.
In the shadow of great rocks, shining with foam and scales,
in the hot shade of the park, the tense language of your embrace
some movement of possibility begins
a smear of yellow paint, a meaning.

III
The nature of this body, cradled
in saltwater warm as sunlight, in
the weightless movements of your arms.

At a fence near the shore, three women
light candles at night, private, secretive
kneeling by dangerous elements. There are
the lights of ships on the black ocean.
Small fires burn in the streets, one doorway
pink with ribbons and children, in motion,
ice cream and cake beside cars in the garage. This is all
the exact name of something we have always known.

These rocks are inhabited, full of eyes
in the fine salt spray, the fishermen's brown and golden hair.
The history of this body, the progress of water.

I walk through sleep and waking, fall
in the safety of this green mineral sky
our hair in damp strands, throat stinging.
Three women are kneeling in volatile air
red and white candles, this secret prayer, this memory (if I
remember one moment only, it may be this
black ocean at our feet
and distant lights, sharp elements on my fingers,
lemon and salt).

This body travels
at rest in the waters, reflecting light
cradled in holy space.

IV

I say, *White ships, arriving.* The green shore and red
bricks of this wall, leaning in brightness.
I say, *there are warnings to be delivered,*
signals and visions in the night, for no new world
is a simple thing.

Morning, Christmas, coffee and chocolate, the rich light
folding around our hands.
Brown waves break hard on the sand. On scraps of paper
I write of white ships, a man who holds a baby beside the ocean,
blue lights, flickering lights.
We walk under trees, we are tossed
in fast ambitious water.

I say, stone walls and crayoned names, location. I have known
these messages from long before, take note, remember.
Hours are shifting, time the colour of sand. The ships
are arriving, always, confused, bearing gold, bearing nutmeg and lyrics.

At night, women change flowers in the church. Scorched figures, angels,
subtle instructions, *rejoice.*
We travel on this white ship with crackers and cheese
in the grey wind of passage.

V

As for the streets, these flowers.
As for the sun, these hands.

In a city of painted walls, elegant, nervous, hot
and brilliant with images, we encounter the day.
The crumbling golden light sustains us, smell of sweet water,
broken pavements, stepped streets, wrought iron.
This incense of cities, Tacuari, Suipacha, Callao.

And I do not ask more than a simple knowledge,
milk for the children, biscuits and miracles.
The heat surrounds us, oil and salt on my skin.
These are the white days, wisp of pink cloud in the evening,
the feast of innocence and a rain of paper.

As for the air, these white scraps flying.
As for the night, this faith

that nothing which has been loved can wholly die
that the heart creates itself daily, and
that our tatters and art, our silk and garbage,
lead us, without complication, without regret
to this small place of light.

VI

Storm on the beach, black bulkheads of racing clouds,
sand whirling against our skin, this saltwater
wild and passionate, laughing.

Here is a moment, a tangled sensation made
from cream and candied almonds, red berries,
the sting of the ocean in my throat,
the burning sun and cold wind, fireworks, silence.
Time moves, changes. No street stays the same
from dawn to noon.

And we move, transient.
Through the deserted streets and shuttered doorways
bodies suspended in water and time.

At the bus station, curled in a plastic chair,
I read papers in foreign languages, rest in the flashing codes
of Christmas trees and pixels, video screens.
This multitude of glory.

Night is a soft hand, etching towns and bodies
in luminous silhouette, the length of this rough country.

VII
The edge of a knife, the sun creates the morning.
The marsh exists
like silver shards of mirror in black weeds
the sky shot through with red velvet, and
the mist begins to rise.
All night I have been awake on this bus
crossing the border
and now the air is full of yellow and we are lost in clouds.

Aching and tired, eyes sticky with night
I stare out the window, alone among sleepers,
at dawn in the grasslands.

Heat and this water are coming towards us
bearing our names, the language of day and thirst.
Sand underneath my fingernails, dirt in my hair.
The marsh is existing, the clouds advancing through
these yellow valleys of grass.

For all our pains and petty sins
we are a new creation in this light; this moment
the only thing I know in this world
that is something like faith. You sleep beside me.
We are in another country.

Brazil-Uruguay-Argentina

Manerplaw

Disjunctures.
Long plans of the world explain themselves
in time, extension and geography,
myself in green and winter lowlands here, among the floods
this anxious northern country.

Today, Manerplaw fell.

And I am here, not in a place
of any particular meaning, only
the artifice of the twisted trees and swans on the water.

Dark bitter chocolate, the liquid centre
of honey and liqueur, the rain for days, cold wind.
Manerplaw burns in the heat of the Burmese summer.
On a scorched cross of coincidence, saying nothing, I carry
this silent news.

*Yesterday, artillery shelling and ground fighting was intense on
all fronts: the Naw Hta area in the south; around Haw Ma Daw
and Sleeping Dog Hill on the west bank of the Salween; and at
Naw Day Hill and White Elephant Hill on the east bank, where
the junta's troops had crossed the river, only seven km from
Manerplaw.*

*Thousands of Karen have fled across the Moei and Salween
rivers into Thailand. Thai border sources confirmed that* KNU
*leaders, representatives of dissident Burmese groups and
Manerplaw civilians have already deserted the headquarters
and are taking shelter in unidentified locations.*

These Memling women, pale, dramatic, concave
pure as the end of a flood of tears
and their lovely hair.

Ask me what happened here.
Ask me the name of this small country. Memory. War.

Saints Catherine, Barbara, Ursula and the virgins
washed out by grief like plunging water, white with knowledge.
But the Magdalen, distinct, improper, carries loaves of warm bread,
the sign of impossible grace. The dispensation of the angels, forgiveness.

What else can we ask for.
This is a damaged land and I
am neither pure nor knowing.
Delicate figures perch on their toes
in graves of heavy stone.

"These people have no shelter, no medicine and no food," said the
statement. "'Urgent and immediate assistance is requested." About
5,000 refugees who crossed from the Manerplaw area are being
cared for by a number of international relief agencies, said a worker
at the Burma Relief Centre on the Thai side of the border. But about
5,000 others who crossed further north are not receiving any aid
because they have to be supplied via the Salween River, and there is
reluctance to risk attack by Burmese troops on the west bank, said
the relief worker, who asked not to be identified.

It has been for years an awareness, a small
item of thought or point of comparison.
Not really a part of my life (though I was
on the plains at the border, hearing the shells explode,
the speed of the trucks, black uniforms)
or a fact I can answer.
Manerplaw falls. Vukovar, Jajce, cities fall, this is a thing that happens.
And here we are promised
a Fun Tour of the battlefields, Hill 60, Passchendaele.
Oh sister saints, we burn as well.

The comfort of rooms, of coffee by narrow streets,
canals and stone churches, stiff with wet and cold.
The comfort of bread and fish, butter and cheese,
a painting of curtains. On the marshes of fear and temptation
I am a simple stranger, my own slight history
escaping between chilled fingers.

I lie beside you, the slanting window
blind with winter rain, shelter
at the border of blue lights, lines of men at welfare kitchens.

These are pure moments, a wafer of safety, pain and love
melting between my lips, this common meal, *we know this.*
Ursula's golden boats on the same wild ocean.

*Thai forces were moving into the forest-clad mountains opposite
Manerplaw as night fell on Friday to prevent any fighting from
spilling onto Thai soil and to keep the 6,000 Karen refugees from
moving deeper into Thailand.*

*The mountain slopes were studded with small fires as the refugees,
surrounded by their bundles of possessions, cooked whatever food
they had managed to salvage.*

*"We are very sad about the situation at our home," said a young
woman preparing rice on a fire on Sunday.*

As these fields fill with winter floods, the summer hills
are soaked with loss. Sunday, red paper kites soar up like stars,
I meet you, breathless, at the feet of the saints
and this girl cooks rice. I believe her curving forehead, slender hands.

At the fragile centre of the burning world
a woman, scandalous, crying. This is the only
place where we can hope. This careless garden.

Fear (after Claude Cahun)

The body, dangerous, white, tangled
in wires and succulent leaves, the body
starved, manufactured, sexual, present,
coated with gold

I float at the edge of the cliff, I
lie on the sand, the body, naked, obsessive, bald

I bury myself in the garden, by cactus
under the dangling globes of fruit. Red

the girl paints her lips, her nipples, covers her eyes
leans her soft flesh on the bars of the window
poses, mouth wet, limbs random
her head falling down

I did not tell you to do this

I did not ask you to do this

The sea is sick with green, the petals
of the thick sea convulse with green, someone will take
this girl, my mask, my lover

please do not hurt

✣

In the days when I was invisible. When
I did not need safety, being untouched
and luminous in my bones

This is the acolyte
this is the narrow escape of the camera, blood-serious lips
this is the thin place

the times of the china doll

but the body surrounds us all in the end
being empty of sense or mercy
and binds us in golden
binds us in cutting thread

One of these days
I will write about needles

In the end we can never survive
despite the temporary
rescues, a cloth coat, an ordinary woman

so there is no reason to fear the day

you do what you must

And I am not brave, my love, only imprisoned
only
near the pale stone and the light
near your hand
near the shore

This face, then, jewelled
cannot be opened or eaten, this
man is mistaken, this
muscle and sleek skin are not
his to take

Sleep is not possible but it is not
forbidden. Thick with gold paint
and artificial hair, female
I wait (she waits) in the dirt
in the cupboard
for only this time

You have to lose *everything*
for one good thing to come out of this body

Thin flames of crackling paper surround
a dance on the seawall
these aging legs, faster than childhood

The happiest moments of my life
are when I lie

Three Months

There are only short moments of safety.
A glass of milk in the darkness, under these
uncompromising stars,
the bright canals of shadowed cities, cradle dreams.
Love, we can never ask for more than this.

Sleeping, I find a shelter under trees, not knowing
anything else to do except subsist
in single moments, losing faith and finding no other choice
but the jump and fall in the terrible sky.

Within and without, there is nothing but mercy
and this is a hard truth
this is the rock of the chosen, the perfect desert, pleasureless,
where we are blessed and broken, and I,
hurt child in a frightened country, live
with each second of time torn open.
We are embraced by this risk, by this only possible
knowledge

that the world is not a warm place unless
we insist it be so, and our hands and arms have no great strength
but our poor hearts beating, this moment, this moment
are not yet betrayed.

Six Months

We make what peace we can
and where we are. Fluids and longings,
precarious dawns.

The body climbs. Past pine and gravel
and the cold flute of the sea. We cannot
trust this blood, but we live inside it.

The white rock arms at the top of the hill
may be man or woman, saviour or mother, we will
never locate the definite answer
here, or across the water where the black clouds gather.

This is the story of climbing, it
is not about arrival. There is (I am living inside this knowledge)
no such thing as arrival, only
one place
one place.

I dream of theory. Awake, I stand under the rain
in a fierce tide of chemicals, calcium, bones and veins
and the body climbs this hill, above these trees.

I wish to be perfect protection, but this body
cannot stop blood or water or stone, cannot
absorb all pain or illness or
the dangerous sun.
I am one place only, and not the best.
But this body can climb
beneath the arms of an unknown promise
breathing.

Eight Months

It burns us anyway.

Cycling in the rain, I am wrapped in silence
crossing Denmark Hill. The world keeps occurring.
Young men and women
wait in a hot place, and others arrive
on buses, with knives. This is a part of us.

My room is filled with unlit candles,
cold and patient, marking the air
with strands of vanilla and wax. This is a thing
we name memory.
Thin hands, brown eyes explore the gates
at the camera's great distance.

Walking the Walworth Road
carrying movement, considering, we
are of course mostly water, but also
something that burns.

We could be fire. We could
sit by each other, scalding, intent
part of this history.

The telephone's voices are urgent, the lines
of electricity and faith require my presence.
The rain soaks my shoes on concrete walkways.
We are complicit, entwined
with so many stories, implicit with time (though you may be
innocent of this, yet our cells
somehow keep choosing each other).

We could burn each other, save
each other's lives, speeding our blood and milk
keeping this vigil.

Christmas 1996

Before we speak, we choose our angels —
snow and compassion, this difficult season.

The messengers of winter bend their knees
on Jarvis Street, on Bathurst
and bless the acts of flesh; sweat and torn bodies,
the need for tomato soup and bread,
birth and the striving
to keep us all, these frail things, warm.

We are flying hard into our own
uncertain terms
(this woman stands on the ice)
cracking the pavement, longing to sanctify
the small beliefs of our hands
(this light, this street)
in a green time, and the sun growing longer
(this year that my body was food
was warm milk in the night).

What occurs in the child's eyes
over and over, complete, this snow conveyed like smoke.
What occurs. No different from itself,
as time burns away beneath our fingers.

I imagine forms of food, measures of giving.
But having been part of sacrament, still
all I can really do is fall to this pavement, hold this child.
All hungers are real. This is a gift, God's own complete undoing,
anarchy of the light.

My hand in the snow. This is the best that we get.

Emergency Ward, Wellesley/Central, August 1997

The fractioning of bone in golden light, the division
of stone and soft tissue, bleeding in the green grass —
this may be
a strange direction towards contentment, but refuge
is where you find it, and always more than strange.
This is what feels like safety, in one moment, one hallway.
A narrow bed on wheels, a sheet across my legs.

At the corner of this desk, the body and language
negotiate their identity, lifting up
the names of things, the burning in the chest or tingling in the fingers,
towards the light.
We are gathered in this white place, my accidental self
and the community of pain, these citizens of lives
which have come into conflict with asphalt, dry eyes
for whom there is no promise of pretty horses
on any waking in this world.
Fear is a friend in the blood, familiar
as bread and pills on a lonely Friday morning,
a pain in the knee, a sense of loss, confusion of sight.

My daughter stands at the edge of a pond,
and giant orange fish blaze under the muddy water,
her pale hair tangled with sun. Her skin
is almost unbroken. Almost safe.
I cannot ensure this forever.

In my small white bed I travel the hallways, conveyed
by the hands and arms of strangers
and arrangements of energy.
There are pictures of my bones in places
I have never seen.
And far away, and older, there are pages
dealing with my own skin, and the nature of burning.

At the doorway, the wounded come and go.
A crown of snakes and needles descends to bless us
in this electric passageway.
Here is the man who is lost. Here on this street.

Dedications

And what if the face of the living creature appears
in a puddle of blood on the roadside, awful, unblinking, enshrined?
You stretch your hand to the mirror. Your nails
are ringed with white. The dark life of the sand
continues across your skin, the crook of your arm.

Wind in the courtyard.
Can you draw out
your heart on a hook, can you draw out
these longings?
This creature breaks on the hinging tooth of the fence.
They are terrible round about.

Behind the walls of heat and distance
a face stirs in water, a lion, an angel, winged catastrophe.
You cannot speak against this creature, it comes to you
unasked, unwanted, the shape of a human eye.

You cannot make promises anywhere but here
where the head is bowed.
We do not predict the coming of this word among the bloodfall,
                                                                    peace,
or this word in the city, *forget*
or *do not understand* or
follow, this wrong direction, this need.

But this is the place where we are.

Or to pin down these pronouns, to put the words here.
This you, not a stranger,
this me.

This me in winter,
wavering days in strange houses, December rain.
At the rim of the water
the fat swift dancing of a breathing seal, ducking and sliding
under the boats, around (and my sister and I
feared illness, sadness, qualification, but now I think
it was only a gift, it was
itself, was okay).

And I dream
you coming through the doorway, holding the child
this reconciliation, this movement from sleep.

The twist in the chest
can break our best devotions. Still
that moment of waking dream escaping from my fingers
is not quite lost.

What then shall we do in the mornings?

This is the coal against the lips, and not
where we might have asked for it to be,
not where the bright edge of knowledge breaks
but here, but here
and subject to a burning.

That Amsterdam

Thin rivers string the city where I kneel
on cold or summer sidewalks, in a black dress
under the fragrant trees

and time is another country, dividing
this cluttered room
this pale March snow,
this bone, this muscle and the child's gold hair.

These things my hands have carried —
fruit and spoons, tissues and eggs, white bread,
books and smears of fluids, suitcases, pens.
The child in my lap, crying, puddles of sick in my shoes.
The child, warm, perfect as silk, touching my face.

From the green and distant city are only fragments
a lavender sleep four floors above the street,
the mannered fall of rain like lace,
stone bridges and a sense of milk.
It is not where she began, but still this city means,
in its perfect anonymous voice,
something like choice, or history
or simply movement.

The child stamps her feet in a crowded room
and sings of the wolves that dance on the walls, their grey paws,
                                                    their young.
The tiny stones cry out in longing.
The snowdrifts part.

We have travelled more oceans to be where we are
than all the liquids in my cells can comprehend
(knowing that I as well
spilled blood and water onto white sheets, this body emptied
towards some impossible future)
and we, through these long blue hallways
these drying flowers, moving creatures,
are making in the end some place that has a name
so old it must be singular.

The wolves, black fetishes stitched with red
are dancing into their own and difficult narratives.
We are part of this thing.
The child and I turn towards the light. A small match ignites.
These cities are only ours.

The Drowned Girl

I

A single step before the cloud
this pale girl waits, dark hair shifting under the wind,
under her hands, Sophia.
In the rain by Luxembourg Gardens she falls to her knees.

Water bends back to meet the light by this green arch
and I walk downwards, cold.
Or stand in the night, briefly, conveyed,
through Macon Loché, through hills, attending.
Genevieve's dead candle inspects us in absolute black.

Here is my hand, turned upward. Tell me
how to hope in a complicated time, a year of sun on the ocean
and the flash of knives. Here is my hand.

The thin wind threads through narrow hidden gardens
mirrors and water, my own burnt face
proceeding towards me down bamboo stairs. This moment as pure
as perfect as the fall of intended streams.

II

Drinking hot chocolate, barefoot, in a courtyard of gravel and rain.
Sophia moves in our green uncertainty, past the pale official stone;
and one is still and white as marble
by the complex tree that grows from our bones
the *logos* breaking our fingers by the side of the glass.

The girl with dark hair is always turning away
to the wall where angels scramble, escaping, blown into light.
A street falls suddenly down to sea, turquoise, incredible.

Yes. Here is my hand. I repeat this until
a space may open in this time between the wars
and I walk through, being
no longer weeping, the child in my arms, the streets full of sun.

But now I go carefully on the cobblestones.
In a narrow alley, the air is sharp with lavender.

III
Imagined roses on the surface of this water.
Approach an island, in the drift of rain, silent
where her dark face waits, her hair veiled, her eyes still.

Walked on this shore. I did this.

Sophia, peace, shadowed by rivers. Girl by the plunging stairs.
Where I embrace this movement to the cloud.
My hand. Is.

Summer

Desire is a dark bird,
the slow curve of wind on a flat roof, chasing
our breath into silence.

I listen in darkness for rain, gentle as thought.
The intelligence of the night surrounds me, moving upon a single point,
circling the light, the fever at the bone.
Desire stands along the wall and speaks

beyond the tears of heat and the break of the heart at noon, saying

we who are torn in strips from our troubled days
we who plant herbs on the porches on Bathurst Street
we wait for this thing

we who attend the sadness of glassy corners
we who walk quickly, under the trees at night
we who reflect the ships in the lakes beneath us
we wait for this thing

I am shifting as slightly
as this yellow lawn, nothing beside me.
The animal kneels, exhausted.

Wings move across this corner
dry and still
incessant, and my hands with their imagined scars
begin to answer.

Winter

Wind, frozen leaves at the edge of the street,
the pure sugar taste of need.
The once and only perfect moon
reaches towards us, hurt by love, close to our dreaming.

These are the words, the way we rise from sleep.
That we reach out our hands and encounter bread,
white blankets, a lamp.

Or this — bright shells by the water's luminous edge
green yew and stone, the sun
at the foot of a mountain, and a small train travels upwards
in the sharp dark smell of broken herbs.

These are the names of our belief
at the corner of Bathurst and Bloor, our fingers
stretched up like the mouths of birds.
The world is filled with mercy, we are almost
helpless before it, the rain cold on our faces.

And this pale flower, appearing on the street at dawn,
out of our bones and the burning night. We are waking
into a stranger morning than we know.

Spring Funeral

In this branched corridor, damp earth
and rain behind windows.
We will not buy honey and eggs by the side of the road.

My feet crunch gently on the glassy sea, as soft and white as milk.
We cast down the work of our hands and enter silence, we
are fed with thin spoons at the gathering of souls.

And the child says, *remember nothing.*

Beyond the singing glass, an unimaginable
broken green (and when birds dream
they do not dream of flying but of song
the small arc of the skull electric with language).

Shall we then walk in these scented fields?
Who will cradle our heads, and who
will wrap us in blue cloth? Our very bones are grass
and our hearts the bread of loneliness, oh *eleison.*

In summer the child and I
perch over the water, at risk, precise.
A swan sleeps below us like a breath of fire.
Yellow flowers pour from the sky, cover our heads, our hands.

Everything falls away.

Ramelau (East Timor, September 1999)

And when Pharaoh drew nigh, the children of Israel lifted up their
eyes, and, behold, the Egyptians marched after them.

I
Pale walls on fire.

At night I am on the floor, on my knees,
the world become voices, my blood stretched tight through my skin,
and the flames are climbing, guns on the battered streets.
Weep on your knees, the darkness breaks
and I am not sometimes anywhere as
one heart splits open. A hundred small white birds, my knowledge
rises and scatters.

Here is one man in the yard of a church, in the dirt.
The fragile bones of neck and wrists stretched out.
A grenade splits open the door.
The blood pours down the final step. The wind passes over.
Red flowers by sapphire water.

The dead come down from Ramelau
and take us in their arms.

II
They are entangled in the land,
the wilderness hath shut them in.

Where shall I walk, where shall I rest
who have no sea or mountains, under the green trees,
my life at a distance?
Where shall I walk, clutching my telephone, helpless?

I shall cup my faith in my hands like a blue and fragile egg.
The flames of this morning
are travelling into the heat of space, locations marked.
Cardboard and coffee, everything burns.

The most poor of the children,
inheritors of the land, oh God,
we could not wish to be so close
to this your exile.

Upon the small earth, the women go on their knees
clutching a shoe, a plastic bottle, a piece of cloth.
A boy kneels down at the foot
of a mountain on fire. He turns to the darkness.

III
Tata Mai Lau, witness this night.
The night they ran to the walls.

The desperate ones of God are beating at the gate,
are sliced by wire, legs torn, their hands a feast of nails.
This is the last kind of prayer we may know,
a rush at the fence, the children screaming.
The eyes of that girl will never leave you. This night
is where we must always live.

I shall lift up mine eyes to the hills.
The city is a cloud of black smoke, oil on your skin.
In Odemau Atas, the men are weeping.

Shall a child raise her hand and the oceans part?
The leaves of the little trees will turn towards us and receive
all we will ever know.

IV
We crawl through blood and water, and our goal,
the small cold rain of love upon the mountains,
walks before us.

The boy comes down from the hills alone, a world in his arms.

In the palm of my hand the histories converge —
slivers of glass, thin threads of blood
and the pulse of electrons down the wire, down
a hundred years, in a blue room.

As all things move together, one day
we will know each other flawlessly
and the bones that wash up on the beautiful shore
will be no less beloved.

Digging Up Bones

(for the people of Suai, East Timor)

This is my country. It is winter here.
I cannot simply place my heart
under the purple flowers, as the warm rains wash away the blood.

The joint of a finger rattles across the sand
and in this place
I sit on a cold step, early snow
a curtain of lights in the sky.
It is dawn at the world's other arc.
They are digging up bones.

In the dream, a valley of feathers.
  But it is not that way

      & yes we shatter here
      & yes we shall stir the dust with our hands
      (lo, they are very dry)
      calling the wind to the hills.

Across the flat pink sky
a plane moves west.

      Speak to the bones. Oh God
      speak to the bones.

The child walks forward into the pale sting of snow,
in her hand the shell of a chestnut, soft and pulpy,
returning to earth.
I arrange my life in bursts of phosphorus
and the carbon smoke behind my eyes.
Twigs bend with red berries.

      Speak these bones to one.

*September 8, 1999. "… received confirmation from reliable
sources that three Catholic priests, Fr Hilario, Fr Francisco
Soares, an unidentified priest and 3 unidentified Catholic nuns,
who were living in Suai, were executed. It has also been
reported that Fr Luis Bonaparte was allegedly killed. These
killings reportedly took place between Monday September 6 and
Wednesday, September 8. We are making every effort to confirm
the exact day. In the town of Fatumaca, the Catholic Salesian
college was also destroyed by militias. It was reported that most
of the Suai city was burned …"*

The sunlight forms in beads at the edge of the day.

*November 12, 1999. "Intelligence agencies from a number of
countries now think that many hundreds, if not thousands, of
bodies have been burnt and dumped at sea or buried in mass
graves over the West Timor border … In recent weeks more and
more bodies have washed up on East Timor's northern and
southern coasts."*

✦

The great trees starve in Suai
their roots stretched into emptiness, the green leaves falling.
The sun in purple clouds desires the sea.

I am not beneath these trees.
I wake from a dream of cut hands and lost bodies
as my daughter moves down the hallway,
small sound in the dark.

Beside the turquoise sea these bones
shall scatter, weeping. We will not know
the names of the fragments, which was a child, which one had
                                                    travelled
long beyond fear.

This scar on my wrist, a shard.

Midnight

Lully lullay, thou little tiny child
by-by lully lullay

This father comes in at the door.
In his hands a baby.
In his hands a gun.
This father dies.

And there is such light in things,
shattering out of the rock, out of the waking sea.
Sanctus, our hope, it is not untrue.
But this father cries for his child's salvation
and dies on the floor. When the baby falls
what hands can lift it to the burning praise of morning?

A human voice, perfect and clean,
skates up from the roof to the pale blue of dawn.
Our love could kill us all, bending over this tiny child, longing for safety.

You shall say to that mountain, remove
and it shall be.
But we falter, our arms imperfect to save,
to hold this one in the fears of his night.
He turns, his eyes alive with pain, into
the violent pulse of blood, or the deep violet flowers
bursting across the water.
The baby's sweet hair beneath his chin, his whole heart shattered.

Kneel on the icy sidewalk, seeking
our heart's desire, a child delivered from pain, all things made gentle.
Shall it be well? Shall the day break softly,
the morning weep at our beauty?

My daughter sings in a rocking chair
oh my love
oh my poor love.
The sky turns round this earth, knowledge upon us, our broken breath.

Shells and Bones

There is no one to speak to.

By the side of the road thick water, a bowl of heat.
And the great fish dead, their creamy skulls breaking out of the flesh.
The kingdom of shells and bones.

A woman throws back her head.

The curve of her throat in the morning. Each moment
the world's first border, edge of the sea, of waves precise beyond voice.
And these yellow roses dying, unremarkable, their smell of green and
sugar in the air.

Hand turns. Is turning in wind.
There may be a mountain. At the border a mountain, not always.
But there may.
The curving flesh of the rocks cut through by road.
Walking beside a road we may understand loss.

As if egg-white and pulsar.
We will not fall to the road. We will not fall again. The roses,
red at their edge like a spot of blood.
The gentle burn of belief, trees shocked into crimson. The air breaks, and
history begins. The means by which we harm each other.

A wind blows through the world, the lift of this woman's head.

Marthe Poems

Marthe, wife of the painter Pierre Bonnard and the subject of his greatest works, suffered from agoraphobia and probably other physical and emotional illnesses.

One does not always sing from happiness — Pierre Bonnard

I
You begin by saying, *I was standing*
there, it was there,
in a blue dress, in the terror of the morning.
Pearls of the dead, a child on the tips of her toes.

We do not choose to love. It only breaks us
and we obey.

You say, Fear is the weight of the wind. Fear is the first word.
Lean my head by the glass. Air on my skin
is the second word of pain.

I will stand with you at our window for a thousand years.
We will never escape.

II
The water, the bath, this element
your velvet safety from the bitter day.

We walk through the small house naked
our flesh a mottle of peach and white, violet and green
the air hot and close.
My feet in white slippers as delicate as a woman's.

Whose body moves past the bath, who lies
imprisoned in pale grey water, outstretched —
whose hand descends, what rises?

A small cup of coffee. The water laps on white enamel.

Who moves, who fears, who falls back again
soft with despair?

The carpet is blazing with sunlight, crimson and deepest yellow.
We pivot about the window, our candied moments
longing towards the sky.
You stretch out your hand and strike the glass.

III
The morning soaked in orange
your small face creeping from the night, a cup of milk
spotted with blood. One shoulder dissolves
into the loving wall. Like the leaves of the orange tree, the heavy scent
of your left arm's survival, a clump of hair.
What more can I do?

I will cover your flesh with paint like the gold of your robe,
assume this other life, unbroken sight.
I will carry your heart in my hands.

Or at the bright table of afternoon
your head turned away
I will crawl on my fingertips through white lead,
the ripe cheese oozing across the plate, that female smell,
past the high platter of vivid plums
to the place where you bend, mixing food for the dog at the edge
of vision,
a silver spoon.

IV
You say, *there is hope of recovery. It may yet be.*
One day I may rise from this water
not like some other thing, but simply
like a woman, like myself. I may put on
a slip, a dress, a coat, a hat. May open the door.

I paint the pink road below the house, open and wide.
In your dream you walk beyond the almond tree, towards the hills.

All that you have as doctor, I outline your muscles
record the labours of your blood, the contraction and expansion of
                                                    your heart.
I bring you tea and taste the acid sweetness on my tongue.
Your short hair floats in the water. The day decays.
The road like a sea at sunset. Gold
is everywhere. Everywhere.

You say to me, *Look. Look now. Do you see*
that blue in the corner of the sky, so cold? That sky
is the next beginning of fear.

The almond tree rises from the red earth.
The little dog and I
walk down the road to the violent sapphire sea.

(I hope all will be well. We must be patient.)

V
Balcony
Marthe
Window
Marthe
Table
Marthe
Radiator
Marthe
Coffee-grinder
Marthe
Mirror
Marthe
Hairbrush
Marthe
Bowl
Marthe
Door
Marthe
Chair
Marthe
Cabinet
Marthe

The meaning of words

VI

This is the man with no face.
The eyes stitched shut and swollen. Awake all night. Afraid.
The head is a piece of meat, red, fat with exhaustion,
the bones are bread and vinegar,
this naked man, his ribs shaking with cold.
Raise the fists in the mirror on poached wet arms. Drop
the head down. Drop it down in
the thick burned hands.
This is the man.

This is the face of love till the end of time.

VII
Coffee?
Could we have coffee?
Could we have a small piece of fruit on a plate?
You lean uncertain by the bathtub,
your feet dipped in the liquid gold of sun. You turn, and the wall
beside you
collapses into the dazzling white of disappearance.
I look out the window.

We can make this beautiful.
There is really no choice.

There is only the skin of light that wraps itself round your shoulders,
the softness of paint and space.
Your face, spinning
behind this bright wheel of need.

My heart beats in an empty room
a shimmer like sunrise, like blood, that moves on the ceiling.
You walk carefully to the mirror.
I turn towards you.

I always turn towards you.

Documents for Artists

after Eugene Atget

An image in brown.
At the end of the street, before the vanishing point
you may see these things:
>   a dark-haired child, running to the curb
>   or grey birds in a scatter over the sky
>   or a shell exploding, fire.
Each of these things is here.
And the light walks into all places, Paris and Tetovo, every hillside.

The photographer perched on the wet roof of the church
foot braced on a flying buttress, the curved lens turned
towards one small gargoyle, chipped at the edges.
In the shabby courtyard below him, rain
a wooden box of flowers
and the mother of God.
Inside, among the ink-thick shadows,
a single pillar twists like a braid of hair,
a discrete and tiny earthquake among the pews.

Or by the green river, the camera travels down the quay,
the deserted quay, the sign on the boat that says CHOCOLAT.
It travels closer, and there is a woman
dressed in black, kneeling.
Her back is turned, her head
falls low to the cobblestones. The camera travels, the lights breaks in two
and you are
where the woman was.
You see everything.
There is no explaining this.

Today the quay is underwater, fences and trees
outlining its body in the brown flood.
Sleep, says the water. *I will cover your face with my hands.*

And this is me.
I am a stranger in a room full of babies
(they are good babies, calm, their plump legs smooth)
an old bad mother with unwashed hair.
I am seeing these things. I am walking like rain
in the pale green room.

In a restaurant off Montmartre
a madwoman, small and fat like a mushroom, is singing.
Curved iron railings reach up, reach down.
She sings in the doorway, wrapped in brown sweaters,
as the crystalline evening falls.
As all things fall.

The photographer paces the edge of the city.
Small and alone, in a heavy coat, he measures the streets for a time of war.

little dead things

how the cloud rises up from the city
oh my love
how the bodies fall through the air

there are so many little dead things

✢

she says, there will be a wind, there will be
a great wind tomorrow

objects in motion,
the wind, the papers travel
with traces of blood and proper names

it goes dark like snow, it all
goes dark like snow

objects descend to the world's magnetic heart

✢

and bodies return to us

they always do

bodies return as a handful of teeth
return as ash
a man stands in the street

grey dust on his shoulders, around his feet
a man in a hat, a shy-looking man,
puzzled, solemn, he finds a piece of paper

he picks it up and reads

✢

the small bones of birds
meaning: death from the air

it is not clear where this is happening, this
is happening everywhere

all those people on the mountain, I saw
all those people, hands and knees, climbing the rocks,
I don't know, they were
old people sick people, these were the women and such,
the men, I don't know, the young men, they go
other places, there are other things
that happen to young men,
this is always the way things are

dawn in a distant place
these houses are burning
while warriors move in an absence

a yellow mountain

small girl, blood on her face

parts of a leg in the desert

there is fear at the pass, the birds like living bullets,
eddies of wind, beings that fly and fall

sit in the dust
and number the little dead things

hold them in your guilty hands

there is not much left to be known
except that we are here
we are all here

the world is a single place

and there shall be rumours of war
and we shall attend in the dust

what sign will there be
when all these things shall come to pass?

Miserere

You walk to the edge of the lake, snow in the air,
a negligent, cannibal soul. Here at the rise of the grey water.
Lift in your hands the cold, lift in your hands
the bright chill of longing.

For the world will never love you as you need.
Beyond these waters, human flesh
will light itself on fire.

You wake in the night to a woman shouting,
but this is another house, not yours, this anger, her feet in the snow,
the story of someone else. You listen to wind.
Cut your finger on glass, your blood is thin.

Dream of a white sail, the sun that lies graciously down.

And once upon a time you held your pain
against you like warmth, like a blanket of knowledge.
Once you could sing like that, velvet and crimson.
You stand at this edge.
Command these stones, and they will turn to sorrow.

On your forehead, a mark like the print of a thumb,
a mark like the dumb identity of dust.
Strike your foot on a rock. Let the bruise form.
Trust in it, this body's moment. At the side of the lake
water returns to water.
Black ash in the sky, from each individual place,
gathers like one.

One Building In the Earth

And she, as the light of the creature slides between her fingers,
barefoot in a small room, the forest outside her.
She is not moving, her heart
is thrown from a cliff, her heart
is weightless. The young moon eats soft bread of absence
from her spoon.

Green leaves scattered across her bed —
in the darker water
the whales slick in the light, their teeth hung with flowers.

Here is the worm of heaven, kneeling,
carnivore head tipped low.
And what shall we do with this power and this need?
To make a white rose break from poison skin,
to gather in the lonely, even
onto our individual blood, my darlings.

Out of the body, dark fluids, thin and dripping, and
the cold wind in the trees. May she have nothing.
May the smell of milk and salt surround her
over the pools of night.

We turn the corner into the great desire, *that all things are saved.*
Hearts stitched together, broken and bad
all things return.

Out of the split heart of matter, a woman is walking.
Perhaps it will happen like this — we will fall to the grass
and the grass will not reject us.

Faith is asleep in our arms like the weight of the sun.

acknowledgements

Poems in this collection have been reprinted from *Because the Gunman* (Lowlife Publishing, 1987), *Eden* (Oberon Press, 1987), *Talking Prophet Blues* (Quarry Press, 1989), *Graffiti for J.J. Harper* (Lowlife Publishing, 1991), *Eating Glass* (Quarry Press, 1994), and *The City on Wednesday* (Lowlife Publishing, 1996). Some poems have been slightly revised for this book.

Alert readers may notice that I have included nothing from my first two books, *Walking Through Fire* (Turnstone Press, 1981) and *Tongues of Men and Angels* (Oberon Press, 1985). I wrote *Walking Through Fire* when I was eighteen years old, and probably should have refrained from publishing it. While I have fewer regrets about *Tongues of Men and Angels*, it is made up of two long narrative sequences that do not excerpt well, and didn't seem significant enough to reprint in full.

Some of the new poems have previously appeared in the following periodicals: *Angel Exhaust* (UK), *Arc, Descant, Grain, Malahat Review, New Quarterly, Queen Street Quarterly,* and *Rampike.* Poems have also appeared in the anthologies *Written In the Skin* (Insomniac Press) and *Stop and Search* (Blue Nose Press, UK). Thanks to Fat Albert's Coffeehouse; St Thomas's Anglican Church; Kevin Connolly, Jason Sherman and *what* magazine; Stuart Ross, Nick Power and the others around the Toronto Small Press Fair; maria erskine, Steven Heighton, David Helwig, Nancy Helwig, Simone Helwig, Tim Lilburn, Ken Simons, David Webster, Bob Wiseman; and to Michael Holmes and Jack David at ECW Press.

Also thanks to the Toronto Arts Council and the Writers' Reserve program of the Ontario Arts Council for financial assistance.